Yoga Fart

A Play in One Act

By Gabriel Davis

gabriel@alumni.cmu.edu
gabrielbdavis.com

Cast
3 w, 1 m

Characters
(In order of appearance)
Amy
Frannie
Peter
Zelda
Stinky Yoga Woman
Male Yoga Instructor
Female Yoga Student
Female Yoga Instructor
Gluteus Maximus
Westchester Lady
Stinky Yoga Guy
FLY Yoga Teacher
Shelley

All male characters can be played by the same actor.

Frannie, Stinky Yoga Woman, Female Yoga Student, Shelley can be played by the same actress.

Zelda, Female Yoga Instructor, Westchester Lady, FLY Yoga Teacher can be played by the same actress.

Time & Setting
Present day, Manhattan. Settings are fluid throughout the play, shifting between various Yoga Studios, a Café, Amy's Subconscious, Amy's Apartment and a Wedding Venue (Bridal Changing Room).

(Spotlight up on Amy; she is at a Yoga class in Warrior 1 position)

AMY

(Addresses to audience)

I came to Yoga to unwind. So far it's not working.

(Moves into Warrior 2)

So I ate a big breakfast, not a genius move. 'Cause I'm really gassy. I've been clenching my ass for the last hour. And breathing into my lungs, which apparently is incorrect because the instructor keeps saying things like …

(Reverses her Warrior)

…. "breathe into your hips", "breathe into the backs of your thighs", "breathe into the tips of your toes." And I have no idea what the hell she's talking about.

(Lowers herself down into Chaturanga)

I feel like I'm flunking Yoga.

(Pushes up into Upward-Facing Dog)

I'm terrified I'm going to let one rip. I can't allow it. I won't allow it. My ass may be tired, it may be shaking, but it is not a quitter. It's a Gladiator.

(Pushes into Downward-Facing Dog)

C'mon Gluteus Maximus, KEEP CLENCHING!!!!!

(Blackout.)

(Spotlight back up, Amy's sitting cross-legged now. Whispers to audience)

This Yoga class is winding down. We're meditating now.

(Closes her eyes, takes a breath in and out. Eyes open)

I'm practicing Loving Kindness Meditation. My sister's wedding is tomorrow and I really, really want to be in a totally loving, happy place for her. Because no matter what she's done, I can't betray the thousands of hours we spent as kids dreaming about our weddings. This is a big fucking deal, and I'm not going to screw it up for her.

(Closes eyes)

I'm going to crush this Loving Kindness Meditation. Dear sister, I'm going to love the shit out of you. Dear sister, I'm going to take my loving kindness and bury you in it.

(Opens eyes)

I'm not sure if I'm doing this Loving Kindness Meditation right.

(Beat)

I love my sister, I do. We've always been so close. I'm her maid of honor. It's such an honor. I'm just struggling right now with the fact that she's a massive slut. See, she slept with my idiot boyfriend Peter after her bachelorette party last night. Peter's not the brightest, so I made sure to give him clear instruction: "give her a ride home." Not take her home and give her a ride. As a police officer he should know better.

(Light comes up on Frannie on mat next to her)

FRANNIE

(Whispers)

Isn't he a stripper?

AMY

Who dressed as a police officer last night! He needs to respect the badge.

(To audience)

This is my Yoga friend, Frannie.

FRANNIE

You had your stripper boyfriend work your sister's bachelorette party?

AMY

I got a friends and family discount. What? Those guys are expensive! I'm not made of money.

(Beat, back to audience)

So my moron boyfriend Peter comes home after and he tells me about it, like he deserves a medal of honor.

> (Spotlight up on Peter, wearing an overly tight police officer uniform)

PETER

Guess who I just did?!
    (Beat)
What's wrong, babe? Oh! Don't worry; I'm not charging extra for that. I know you're on a budget, babe.

AMY

Why would you do that?

PETER

Uh, because it feels good giving back and I think donations are tax deductible and she seemed so sad about getting married. She was crying.

AMY

So you just thought why not give her a pity-pity bang-bang?

PETER

Well, not at first. I was like asking myself "what can I do to make her stop crying?" "What can I do?" And suddenly the answer just popped out at me. Which happens with tear-away pants.
    (Beat)
Because the answer was my dick. Because it physically popped out.

AMY

Yes, we get it.

PETER

And I was like, "hey dude, you're up late! Well, as long as you're up, you might as well do some good in this world."

AMY

Wow. That's …. You're like Saint Peter the Cheater.
    (Lights off Peter, actor exits. Amy is breathing loudly in and out now and very quickly.)

FRANNIE

    (Trying to get Amy to pace herself)
Breathe in, 1 2 3 4 5, and hold, 1 2 3 4 5, breathe out, 1 2 3 4 5.

AMY

This Loving Kindness Meditation isn't working, Frannie, I feel furious.

FRANNIE

Just observe the feelings, don't judge them. We're about to Om. Maybe the Oming will help.

    (Entire class begins to Om together. Amy Oms but continues too long and too loud after everyone else has stopped Oming).

AMY

    (To audience)
I always feel like I'm Oming too long. Like my Om is the last Om at the party, still lingering after everyone else's Om has gone home.

FRANNIE

Amy, pay attention, it's time to …

    (Hands at heart center)

AMY AND FRANNIE

The divine light in me honors the divine light in you.
    (Beat)
Namaste.

AMY
Well, Frannie, that wasn't calming at all. And now I have to go meet my sister for coffee and I have no idea how I'm going to calmly talk about this with her and forgive her and then love her again so her big day can be perfect.
    (Beat)
I can't. I won't. I'll bury my feelings. Push them down deep!

FRANNIE
Sounds painful.

AMY
I just spent the last hour holding all the air in my body while twisting it like a balloon animal. I can keep my shit together for one more day until the wedding is over.

    (Blackout. Lights up, Amy is sitting opposite her sister Zelda)

ZELDA
Oh, coffee is good. It's good.
    (Smelling it, then sipping it, then chugging it)
Mmmmm, coffffeeeeee.

AMY
If you wanted to sleep in …

ZELDA
No it's fine, I'm fine. Just … boy do I feel hung over. We all got pounded last night, huh?

AMY

Some more than others.

ZELDA

Good call on planning my party for last night instead of the night before. I can only imagine having to get married right after last night. But it was absolutely perfect, Ames, just a wonderful night that I'll never forget so long as I live. My last hurrah as a single woman. I can honestly say I went out with a bang. Thank you, Amy.
    (Beat)
Ames? Amy? Are you listening? You look far away.

AMY

I'm just practicing my Yoga breathing. And out, 1 2 3 4 5.

ZELDA

Ugh, I haven't done Yoga in ages. And I could use it. I think I threw my back out last night from … dancing so much. But it's just not safe to practice Yoga in the city anymore. Not with that "Farting Yogi" still out there.

AMY

Farting Yogi?

ZELDA

There's this blogger in the city, she calls herself "The Farting Yogi." No one knows what she looks like, or who she actually is. She visits Yoga classes and fart-bombs them. Then calls out people on her blog who are not Zen with her nasal pollution. Like she must have hidden cameras because she puts pictures of people up on her blog practicing Yoga and looking horrified and grossed out. No one has been able to catch her.
    (Beat)

And it's possible they never will, because she's like started a movement. So you never know for sure if you're smelling The Farting Yogi herself or one of her followers.

                        AMY
I'm not aware of her.

                        ZELDA
You've been lucky. The last Yoga class I went to …
    (Zelda moves over to a mat, next to her is a Stinky Yoga
    Woman in Downward Dog position)
I'm pretty sure she – or one of her followers – was directly to my left. This lady's Downward Dog smelled like Downward Dog doo-doo. That's when our instructor says …

(Lights up on Male Yoga Instructor)

                MALE YOGA INSTRUCTOR
Alright, now come into Sukhasana and take a deep breath in.
    (Everyone comes into cross-legged position)
We're going to practice Kundalini breathing.

                        ZELDA
And I'm like, "Noooo."

                MALE YOGA INSTRUCTOR
Breath of fire.
    (He starts practicing breathing in and our rapidly).

                        ZELDA
My nose feels like it's on fire! I try to breathe out of my mouth instead, but the instructor locks eyes with me and says …

                MALE YOGA INSTRUCTOR
Breath of Fire must flow through the nose. Now breathe! Breathe! Do not let anything break your focus, your Drishti.

MAINTAIN YOUR DRISHTI!

　　　　　　　ZELDA
I'm trying, I'm trying! But the smell of shitsky is breaking my Drishti!
　　　(Beat, to Amy)
I peer around the room and I'm not the only one. A few people are actually getting up with their mats and leaving. The instructor looks a little concerned …

　　　　　MALE YOGA INSTRUCTOR
Today, I'd like to talk about the foundational Yogic principle of Ahimsa or First, do no harm. One lady says loudly:

　　　(Actress playing Stinky Yoga Lady puts on different hair tie or something to become Female Yoga Student. She runs to another spotlight in the studio; maybe give her a thick New York accent)

　　　　　FEMALE YOGA STUDENT
Tell that to whoever is harming our noses!

　　　　　MALE YOGA INSTRUCTOR
In Yoga, we extend compassion to our fellow beings. We put ourselves in their shoes. If the smell in here seems harmful, imagine how holding that smell inside must have felt.

　　　(Amy raises her hand, he points at her).

　　　　　　　AMY
Perhaps painful?

　　　　　MALE YOGA INSTRUCTOR
Very good.

　　　　　FEMALE YOGA STUDENT

Fuck this!

(Spotlight off the lady)

ZELDA
The lady storms out. A few more people follow her. You gotta give it to that instructor, he just continues:

MALE YOGA INSTRUCTOR
Today, let's support each other. Let's not keep our painful, smelly winds inside. Let's do the Wind-Relieving Pose together to release them!

ZELDA
And then he demonstrates the Wind-Relieving Pose.

AMY
Huh, I've never seen that one.

ZELDA
Basically, you lay on your back and use your leg as a pump to force all the farts out.

(He's now in the position)

MALE YOGA INSTRUCTOR
(To audience, big smile on his face as he demos the Wind-Relieving Pose)
LIKE THIS!!

ZELDA
The sounds and smells that ensued were nothing short of horrible. I look over to the woman on my left.
(Spotlight or area light back up on the Stinky Yoga Woman)
She's smiling broadly. She was enjoying it!

(Beat)
I didn't want to be one of those non-compassionate people who stormed out. I was determined to stick in there with whatever this was becoming. I tried. I tried to accept everyone's farts. I repeated our instructor's words:

MALE YOGA INSTRUCTOR
(Still doing the Wind-Relieving Pose)
May all beings be happy, may all beings be free.

ZELDA
I told myself, we are all one, I am in everyone's farts and everyone's are in mine. I tried to lose track of where my farts end and everyone else's begin. I tried to be one with the farts and accept them. But I didn't.
(Zelda gets up and begins to move away)

MALE YOGA INSTRUCTOR
Where are you going?

ZELDA
My path to enlightenment will not be paved with farts!!!
(Exits the class to a foyer area, the Stinky Yoga Woman follows behind her)

STINKY YOGA WOMAN
Excuse me. I couldn't help but notice you seemed troubled in there by my *ass*halations. Here.
(Hands Zelda a flyer.)

ZELDA
(Reading it)
The FLY Yoga Studio?

STINKY YOGA WOMAN

Farting Laughing Yogis Yoga Studio. It's a safe space where one can let loose among like-minded folks.

ZELDA

Not my folks.

STINKY YOGA WOMAN

It's really quite freeing, for the mind and booty.
> (Slaps her own butt. Suddenly pulls out a pocket watch)

Oh, I'm late!

AMY

She had a pocket watch?

ZELDA

> (To Amy)

I know, right? Who carries a pocket watch?
> (Stinky Yoga woman hurries out still looking at her watch)

AMY

And with that, the Smelly White Rabbit disappeared down a Fart Hole and little Zelda followed her down it.

ZELDA

Shut up! I did no such thing.

AMY

You can totally tell me if you joined a Fart cult...

ZELDA

Oh enough about me, what about you? What about this boyfriend of yours?

AMY

What about him?

                    ZELDA
Ok, I'm just going to come out and say it.
          (Beat)
He's not for you. I got to know him a little bit, on the ride home last night. Not a lot upstairs. Where do you see him and you in say, five years, you know?
          (Beat)
I mean, I get it. The sex is probably amazing, right? I mean I'm just guessing … how did you meet again?

                    AMY
We actually met at his work. I was putting a 20 down his pants and we just connected, so I asked him "what time do you get off?" And he's like "Right now. But I get done with work at 11."

                    ZELDA
Ewwww.

                    AMY
Yeah, I was totally turned off, I mean, I hate waiting for people. But I waited. Because he's a good guy. When he's not stripping, he actually devotes himself to Special Ed.

                    ZELDA
He's a teacher?

                    AMY
A student. He works real hard but …

                    ZELDA
… but mainly you're just addicted to his shlong, am I right?
          (Beat)

You don't have to answer that, but the point is – it's like I'm worried about you. Like when you got really into Krispy Kreme donuts and gained all that weight. Thank the Lord they closed all those stores to avoid bankruptcy, you know, otherwise where would you be today? Maybe diabetic.

AMY

I don't want to talk about this with you, Zelda.

ZELDA

If you can't talk to your own sister about this stuff, who can you talk to? You know just because I'm getting married sweetie, nothing is going to change. I'm still your big sis. I'm here for you. Can you open up to me?

AMY

You want me to open up to you?

ZELDA

Yes. Always. I want you to be honest about how you're feeling about all of this with me.

AMY

You want ME to be honest with YOU.

ZELDA

Ames, are you OK?

AMY

I'm running late. I've got a Yoga class in 15 minutes.

ZELDA

Another one? How many are you doing in a day?

AMY

As many as it takes.

ZELDA

You seem upset.

AMY

You know, being a maid of honor is stressful. But I want to be perfect for you tomorrow. I'm in the home stretch, Zelda. And the Yoga this morning did not help me decompress. It did not help me decompress at all. So I'm going to do more Yoga. Now. I'll see you tomorrow.

ZELDA

Amy!
    (Lights out on Zelda)

AMY

You know, in New York City, there is literally a Yoga class happening every hour of the day and night. If that's what it's going to take to keep me from going ape-shit on my big sis before her wedding, then for the next …
    (Checking her watch)
… 22 hours, in the city that never sleeps I will become the Yogi that never sleeps!

    (Area light up on Male Yoga Instructor. As he calls out the positions, Amy moves through them)

MALE YOGA INSTRUCTOR

Put UP your Dog. Put DOWN your Dog. Three-legged Dog. FLIP that Dog. Dolphin Dog! CARROT DOG!

    (On "Carrot Dog" she looks up a little confused. He actually pulls a carrot dog out of his pocket and begins eating it. Area light down on Male Yoga Instructor. Area light up on Female Yoga Instructor)

FEMALE YOGA INSTRUCTOR
Alright ladies, I'm going to shout and you're going to twist!
TRIANGLE POSE! AND TWIST. AND TWIST.
SIDE ANGLE POSE! AND TWIST. AND TWIST.
CHAIR POSE. AND TWIST. AND TWIST.

(Area light off the Female Yoga Instructor. Only Amy remains in light. She returns to Chair Pose)

AMY
I've been hopping from studio to studio, class to class. The Zelda situation, plus a big breakfast, plus coffee, plus hours of bending and twisting. I feel a fire within my gut and it's moving toward my butt! Help!
(Area light up on a man dressed as a fireman)

GLUTEUS MAXIMUS
I'm here!

AMY
Who are you?

GLUTEUS MAXIMUS
'Tis I, Gluteus Maximus.

AMY
Why are you dressed as a fireman?

GLUTEUS MAXIMUS
There's a fire raging inside you, Amy. If I allow it to escape there will be a backdraft that could kill everyone in the studio, or worse, gross them out and ruin you socially.

(Loud fart noise)

AMY

Was that me???

                    GLUTEUS MAXIMUS
I have not failed you, my Queen.   It was her!
         (Pointing across the studio at Stinky Yoga Lady, whom
         an area light has just come up on)

                         AMY
She looks so happy.

                    STINKY YOGA LADY
     (Pulls out a pocket watch)
Oh no, I'm late!
         (She scurries out)

                         AMY
After class, people are talking.

         (Westchester Lady and Male Yoga Student are in
         conversation, Amy approaches them)

                    WESTCHESTER LADY
Did you hear that in there?

                    MALE YOGA STUDENT
How could we miss it, it was like a bridge demolition in there.

                    WESTCHESTER LADY
The instructor really should have said something.

                         AMY
With all the twisting and bending it's bound to happen. The classy thing is to just ignore it.

                    WESTCHESTER LADY
     (To Amy)

Would you ever let one go like that in class?

       MALE YOGA STUDENT
 (To Amy)
Yeah, what are you - Pro-Fart?

       WESTCHESTER LADY
I remember when there wasn't tolerance for farting in workout classes. You let one out, you were out. One woman let one out at the Westchester Health Club, her husband was a Wall Street trader. Next day, the Federal Trade Commission, off an anonymous tip, arrests her hubby. They said for insider trading, but everyone knew it was for his wife's inside farting.

 (Frannie comes up to the group)

       FRANNIE
Oh, c'mon, everyone knows it's totally fine and not a big deal to fart in a Yoga class. It's like an unwritten rule that you think about something else and pretend it's not happening. Just like sex with my husband.

       AMY
Frannie! I didn't see you in there.

       WESTCHESTER LADY
Yeah, no, it's tough out there ladies. It's like "you fart, you die."

       MALE YOGA STUDENT
Farting is social suicide.

       WESTCHESTER LADY
It's a nasal assault, it's nose rape. It's like "Stop raping my nose with your farts."
 (Westchester Lady and Male Yoga Student exit)

                        FRANNIE
I'm surprised to see you at the studio today. Isn't your sister's wedding in a few hours?

                        AMY
Oh my God, you're right. The time has flown by. I've been hopping Yoga studios trying, trying to just keep all my lovely, nasty feelings toward the lovely, nasty bride sucked in.

                        FRANNIE
Maybe it'd be better to let them out?

                        AMY
What is that you're holding? Is that a flyer?

                        FRANNIE
That lady with the pocket watch was handing them out to people before class. FLY Yoga Studio. Looks interesting. Their logo looks …
        (They're both looking at it together)
…sort of like a heart with smoke coming out of it.

                        AMY
I think it's the outline of a butt.

                        FRANNIE
They have a class starting in a few minutes.

                        AMY
Are you thinking of going?

                        FRANNIE
I would, but I have a brunch date with the hubby. Here.
        (Hands her the flyer, starts to exit)

                    AMY
          (Calling after Frannie)
I'm not going!
          (Frannie has exited. Amy looks down at the flyer).
Well, maybe I'll just take a peek.
          (Lights down on Amy. Lights up on Stinky Yoga
          Woman standing, pumping the leg of Stinky Yoga Guy
          who is laying down. Basically an assisted Wind-
          Relieving pose. Fart sounds optional. Amy appears at
          the periphery, watching. Stinky Yoga Woman notices
          her)

               STINKY YOGA WOMAN
Oh, hello there. Come in, come in.
          (Looking at her pocket watch)
We're about to begin.

                    AMY
Oh I'm ... I was just peeking in ...

               STINKY YOGA WOMAN
Come join us. I'm Hissy Biscuit and this is Brown
Moonbeam.

                    AMY
I'm ... Amy.
          (Beat)
Is she here?

               STINKY YOGA WOMAN
Who?

                    AMY
The Farting Yogi.

               STINKY YOGA WOMAN

Oh we've never actually seen her.

> STINKY YOGA GUY

Some say she no longer occupies a physical body, that she has ascended to a higher plane –

> STINKY YOGA WOMAN

She released a wind so mighty her entire being was swept up in it.

> STINKY YOGA GUY

And now she is the wind.

> STINKY YOGA WOMAN

Do you feel that breeze?

> STINKY YOGA GUY

That could be her.

> AMY

On my way here, I was checking out her blog. She just posted yesterday. You believe a breeze is typing a blog?

> STINKY YOGA WOMAN

Everyone's belief is different. Some marry the Farting Yogi philosophy with their own faith.

> STINKY YOGA GUY

I break wind for Jesus.

> STINKY YOGA WOMAN

Oh, it's beginning!

(Lights up on FLY Yoga Teacher who addresses the class)

FLY YOGA TEACHER

Before we begin today's practice, I wanted to thank Shelley who has been so gracious to open her Yoga studio to us as a temporary home for FLY Yoga while ours is fumigated. Namaste Shelley.

SHELLEY

Absolutely. To my regulars, consider this as a workshop on tolerance and acceptance. To those here from FLY Yoga, a word on Green Juice and Juice Cleanses. I can't say enough good about them, they make you feel great from the inside out. Green Juices, a body purifier for you and an air purifier for my Yoga Studio. I'll just be selling it over here with the Febreze.

FLY YOGA TEACHER

Uh, thank you Shelley for, um, highlighting for those new to FLY Yoga, that it can be difficult to release some of the things we hold inside. We're afraid if we allow our troubled southern winds to enter the atmosphere, we will find ourselves rejected for them. But we must learn to accept the dark clouds that dwell within us and release them.

We are trumpets, we hold the power to raise our asses in harmony, and sound in a new era where everyone is free to fart.

People say it is unladylike to fart. FLY Yoga says, it is inhuman not to.

So I say to you today, all who may fart follow me. My sisters and brothers. Fart Loudly, Fart Proudly!

>(Lights down on everyone but Amy. Spot on Amy, she addresses the audience)

AMY
As I move through the Asanas, it's a fairly normal Vinyasa practice, actually. No Wind-Relieving Poses or anything weird and, well, I feel relieved. And the second I relax, I feel it, an *ass*halation moving fast to escape.

FRANNIE
I'm here, Amy.

AMY
Frannie! I thought you were at brunch with your husband.

FRANNIE
Oh I am; we decided to brunch in your subconscious.

AMY
You brought your husband to my subconscious?

FRANNIE'S HUBBY
Hi Amy! So, you're thinking of farting on all these fine people, huh?

AMY
I don't know … There are lots of non-cult members here. Normal people, who may not be ready for this. Am I ready for this? To break with everything I know about appropriate public behavior and break wind in public?

FRANNIE
As the great Yogi Shakespeare never wrote:
"Fartlet, Act 3, Scene 1:
To toot or not to toot? That is the question. Whether 'tis nobler in the studio to suffer the twists and bends of a Yoga practice,
Or to break hot wind amongst a sea of Yogis
To let one rip, to clench no more

                    AMY
And by unclench, we say to free the fizzler and the thousand
natural gases that flesh is heir to. 'Tis a consummation,
devoutly to be wished.
    (Beat)
I just don't know, Frannie.

                FRANNIE'S HUBBY
    (Who now has a guitar, playing for Amy)
And how many farts must a Yogi lay down
Before you can call her a Yogi?
Yes, 'n' how many beans must a white women eat
Before she farts in the sand?
The answer my friend happens when you break wind, the
answer is you must break wind.

                    FRANNIE
You can do this Amy, we believe in you.
    (Lights down on Frannie and her husband).

                    AMY
Frannie, Frannie don't go! Oh God. I'm all alone.
    (Beat)
When Zelda and I were little, she stole all my Ken dolls. She
said it was because my Kens weren't good enough for my
Barbies and she was going to get me better Kens. But she
never did. What she did do is have this like, Harem of Kens
who served her Barbie queens. And after awhile I started to
feel really angry about it, and I got so mad that I took all her
Barbie's clothes and flushed them down the toilet and I threw
all the Kens in the garbage. So then Zelda just had all these
naked Barbies. She was so upset, she didn't speak to me for a
week. And I felt so very, very alone. I was convinced she
actually hated me.
    (Beat)

I'm so scared, I'm terrified.
>	(Lights up on Gluteus Maximus)
Gluteus Maximus!

GLUTEUS MAXIMUS
Do not fear, my Queen. For I stand guard at the rear gates defending your honor. Thou smelly dragons shall not escape thine castle and reduce thine kingdom to asses…ashes.

AMY
What if …. if we let the dragons loose?

GLUTEUS MAXIMUS
Let the dragons fly!? Do you have a fever, my Queen? Are you unwell?

AMY
This could make me well.

GLUTEUS MAXIMUS
I cannot allow you to destroy your kingdom.

AMY
Maybe this is what's needed to restore peace to the kingdom.

GLUTEUS MAXIMUS
I swore an oath to protect you. What you're asking-

AMY
>	(She touches his face)
Gluteus. You've served me well, but now your watch is ended. You can take your leave of me.

GLUTEUS MAXIMUS

As you command, my Queen. But before I go ... I have to confess, just as I've dwelt in your bottom all these long years, so you've dwelt in my heart.
    (He dips her back, romantic kiss, he begins to exit)

AMY
Oh Gluteus, my Maximus! Farewell!
    (He is gone, lights down on him)
Ok ... Here goes!!!!!!
    (She closes her eyes. Blackout accompanied by massive loud farting noise that ends up sounding like fireworks and there is giggling from all the actors as the farts fly. Spotlight back up on Amy, as she delivers the monologue she is putting on a bridesmaid dress).
I farted in Yoga class. It was loud. And I didn't die. My heart started pounding but it did not explode. I thought I would be devastated but I was not. Instead something unexpected happened. I laughed. At first a little giggle and then a full-blown belly laugh. In fact, I laughed so hard that I farted again. And again, and again. Embarrassing, no? No. No.

I could feel people staring but I didn't care. I thought I would care. Feel my palms grow clammy, my chest tighten. No. I felt a lightness, wonder, awe. Who knew I had so much air inside me. My body had deflated but my spirit had inflated! I waited for the self-loathing to come. But there was only... Stillness. Silence. Then in that silence, a little voice. I love you. Your body is amazing.

I realized, this was why I'd come to Yoga in the first place. No, not to fart publicly. To fart publicly and survive it. I know, it's unladylike. But in the depth of this indignity, I had found my greatest strength. Here I was looking my fear in the face And believe me, I had feared this moment. I had played it out in my mind. And it always ended with all the ladies around me pulling hidden rocks out of their Lululemon attire and stoning me mercilessly. But not much happened. Here I was staring fear in the face and realizing...it was a bunch of hot air. And I could release it!

I breathed in deep, so deep another loud exclamation of my new found freedom erupted from my behind. "Excuse me," the woman behind me said. "But could you step outside for a moment. Some of us are trying to practice Yoga..." This should have destroyed me. It should have sent me whimpering out of the room. But I felt my calm breath, heard myself say: "Excuse me, but I am practicing my fartnassanas thank you very much."

Then something amazing happened. A little noise erupted from another corner of the room. A few other people giggled, then laughed, and then more noises erupted. And it was beautiful. A symphony of fartnassanas. I was free, they were free. And I realized in that moment...
    (Lights come up on Peter in his cop outfit)
I was free of you, too. You can't hurt me anymore.
    (Beat)
What are you still doing in my apartment, Peter? Get out.

PETER
And go where? I can't afford anything else.

AMY
You make 500+ a night!

PETER

Not anymore. The industry is changing. No one carries cash anymore. The other day, a lady actually asked me if I take credit. So I'm like uh, "yes, I do. Just swipe your card between my balls."

AMY

(Laughing at him)
Is that a secure transaction? Do your balls take chip cards?

PETER

I know, right? But, no. My balls do not take chip cards. What's a chip card?

AMY

I'm sorry, no. Get out.

PETER

But ... why?

AMY

Why?

PETER

Is it me? Is it something I did?

AMY

Don't play dumb, Peter.

PETER

I'm not playing.
    (Breaks down and cries).
I don't understand what's happening.

AMY

You slept with Zelda.

PETER

Should I not have?

AMY

No, no Peter you should not have.

PETER

(Peter begins to cry)
Is she upset? Did I not do a good job?

AMY

No, no that's not ... Peter, Peter, honey. I ... I think the other thing is, if I'm really being honest about us, if I ask myself "Where do I see us in five years" ... I don't. When it comes to you and me, one and one does not make two.

PETER

But one and one ...
    (thinks)
Does make two.

AMY

It's a metaphor.

PETER

Maybe they'll cover that in Algebra next semester.

AMY

Maybe.

PETER

Can we stay together until then?

AMY

See, Peter, the thing is ... there's a part of me that wants to say yes. You know, there's a part of me that really enjoys being with you. Like REALLY enjoys it. But sometimes the things I really enjoy, they're not good for me. Like Krispy Kreme donuts. If I eat too many of those, I could become diabetic. Being with you, it feels good, but ... it could make me diabetic.

PETER

It could?

AMY

Well, I'm no doctor, but I think so. You don't want me to become diabetic do you?

PETER

No.

AMY

Then you'll have to say goodbye. If you love me.

PETER

Goodbye Amy. And I'm sorry about your sister. If I ever get another chance, I'll try to bang her better next time.

AMY

Thanks Peter.
    (Beat)
Well, goodbye, Peter.
    (Lights down on Peter. Light comes up on Zelda in her wedding dress).

ZELDA

Amy! My little sis made it!!!
    (Gives Amy a big hug)

You were running a little late, I was terrified something happened to you. Can you tie this up in the back?
    (Amy does, while she's tying she says…)

AMY
I wasn't going to say this to you today. I was going to hold it in until you got back from your honeymoon. But I don't want to fake my way through your big day. And sometimes its better to just … release the dark clouds, get them out there, and move on.
    (Beat, she's done tying, Zelda has turned to face her)
I know you slept with Peter. He told me.

ZELDA
I see.
    (Beat)
Look I, I know it looks bad but … I was protecting you. I tested him to see if he was worthy of you and he failed.

AMY
Oh, so you altruistically fucked my boyfriend.

ZELDA
Yes.

AMY
Threw yourself on his sword for the greater good.

ZELDA
Exactly!

AMY
So you're like the Mother Theresa of Sluttiness is that it?

ZELDA

I know it seems crazy, but on some level ... I knew it would come out ... partly because the whole time we were ... together ... he was telling me how he hoped he was doing a good job and if I was satisfied with his services, would I please share my positive feedback with you. I hoped he was joking.

AMY
Sadly, he wasn't.

ZELDA
Well, good. So it worked, you found out and now it's only a matter of time before you inevitably break up with him. Which will be great for you!

AMY
It's already done, he and I are done.

ZELDA
You're welcome.

AMY
(Laughing, can't believe it).
You know, Zelda ... before I started practicing Yoga if I found out you slept with my boyfriend ...I might have not shown up today, for you. And left you without a maid of honor on your wedding day. But Yoga teaches faithfulness.

I might have stolen your wedding dress last night and sold it on eBay. But Yoga teaches non-stealing. I might have returned your wedding gift and got myself that Louis Vuitton clutch I've been eyeing. But Yoga teaches non-greed. I might have told you I know, but I don't care and you haven't hurt me. But Yoga teaches truthfulness.

I might have said- "I know you banged my boyfriend. Now you're going to get banged. By my fist in your face."
    (Miming punch)
"Bang." But Yoga teaches non-violence. Instead, I'm just trying to breathe … to hold this incredibly uncomfortable pose and still be here, for you, as your sister, on this sacred day in your life.

Yoga teaches that underneath everything, we are part of the same underlying ultimate essence. And right now, I'll admit, that essence feels pretty bitchy.

But right now, I bow to that essence, to all of this pain, this agony - because you must feel it too, to do something like this.
    (Bowing to her sister)
Namaste Bitch.

                    ZELDA
So now I'm supposed to just walk out there and get married with you thinking I'm a bitch?

                    AMY
Can you honestly with a straight face, tell me you don't think what you've done doesn't qualify you for the title?

                    ZELDA
You know, you have always misunderstood me. Remember that time I took all your Ken dolls?

                    AMY
Oh I remember it.

                    ZELDA

There was a recall that year of those particular Ken dolls, they were dangerious Ames. Grandma said they were real Ken dolls but really they were cheap off-brand knock-offs covered in lead paint... I tried to explain it to you, but you were four. You didn't get it. So I took them, and was saving my allowance to replace them... but I only got a buck a week.

AMY
If they were so dangerous, why did you play with them?

ZELDA
Yes ... yes.. I did enjoy the extra Kens ... OK? But why do you think I was wearing kitchen gloves when I had them serve their Barbie Queens? It was to protect myself from lead poisoning!!!
(Beat)
And have you forgotten how I gained 15 pounds in high school on Krispy Kremes? You were constantly bringing boxes home and I was afraid if I didn't devour them faster than you, you were going to become diabetic.

AMY
Don't make eating my donuts into a good deed.

ZELDA
But it was, oh God, Ames. It was!

AMY
Let's ... let's just walk you down the aisle.

(Beat, Zelda starts crying)

ZELDA
I don't know.

AMY

What do you mean you don't know?

ZELDA

I don't know if I want to.

AMY

What?

ZELDA

If I'm married, I may not have as much time to watchdog your life. You're my little sis. I can't abandon you out here.

AMY

Suddenly being single is "out here." It's not the vacuum of space, it's Manhattan.

ZELDA

I feel like there's this dark cloud that has always sort of followed you around, and if I'm married, I might not be there to blow it away.

AMY

Don't worry ... I ... learned how to blow it away myself.

ZELDA

You did?

AMY

I went to a Farting Yogi cult meeting. They taught me.

ZELDA

That sounds disgusting.

AMY

It was liberating.

ZELDA

I'm also scared of marriage, Ames. Only one man for the rest of my life? When I was a young girl, I always imagined I'd have a whole Harem of Kens.

AMY

Well, you're getting one Ken.

ZELDA

I know, it worked out well; that's his name. But my fear of monogamy ... it's like my own personal dark cloud. Am I going to walk down that aisle and bring that cloud into my marriage?

AMY

No, no you're not. I can help you release it. Lie down. Trust me.
    (Zelda does)
Give me your leg.

ZELDA

The ... Wind-Relieving Pose?

AMY

This might smell.
    (She begins pumping Zelda's leg)

ZELDA

Oooooohhhhh, my God. What is happening right now!
    (Beat)
I love you Ames.

AMY

I love you too, Zelda.

ZELDA

I'm scared.

                    AMY

Let go.

                    ZELDA

It's unladylike.

                    AMY

Real women pass gass, my love.
    (Beat)
It's going to be ok … just let go.

                    ZELDA

Ok.

                    AMY

Ok.
    (Beat)
Let 'er rip, Zeldie.

                    ZELDA

Here goes!
    (Blackout, loud fart noise)

END OF PLAY

Copyright © 2016 by Gabriel Davis

All rights reserved. No part of this play *The Yoga Fart* may be reproduced in any form or by any electronic or mechanical means, including information storage and retrieval systems, without permission in writing from the author, except by a reviewer, who may quote brief passages in a review. Any members of educational institutions wishing to photocopy part or all of the work for classroom use, publishers who would like to obtain permission to include the work in an anthology, or actors who wish to use portions of this play for audition or showcase purposes should send their inquiries to *gabriel@alumni.cmu.edu*

ISBN-13: 978-1523742998
ISBN-10: 1523742992

Printed in Great Britain
by Amazon